Essential
Fashion Design

Essential
Fashion Design

Illustration • Theme Boards • Body Coverings • Projects • Portfolios

Janet Boyes

B.T. Batsford Ltd. London

© Janet Boyes 1998
First published 1998

All rights reserved.
No part of this publication may be reproduced
in any form or by any means without permission
from the Publisher.

Printed in China
for the publishers
BT Batsford Ltd
583 Fulham Road
London SW6 5BY

www.batsford.com

ISBN 0 7134 7699 0

A CIP catalogue record for this book is available from
the British Library.

Contents

Introduction

Essential Fashion Design *aims to equip anyone with basic design skills and an interest in fashion design with the confidence to realize their creative ideas in both two and three dimensions.*

This book covers all the foundation skills needed for fashion design, from basic design exercises through a series of innovative projects to mounting a portfolio and preparing for an interview for a specialist fashion course.

If you are already participating in an art or design course the exercises and projects in this book will provide additional experience which will encourage the development of your ideas and help with final presentation sheets.

Studying fashion is not just about clothing, accessories and their manufacture. Fashion is about design and style and touches upon all aspects of our daily life, influencing the way we live, the furnishings and decor in our homes, the cars we drive, the food we eat, the magazines and newspapers we read and the films and TV shows we watch. Even the way in which we organize our social activities is influenced by what happens to be fashionable at a particular time.

Everything sits within its context. It is impossible to design anything without being conscious of how it relates to the broader issues of society. So, in addition to being aware of what is happening in the creative, visual and the performing arts and in the media, fashion designers must be avid readers of magazines and newspapers and regular visitors to museums and exhibitions. Architecture and natural landscape are also of immense importance as areas for study.

If you have decided that you will study fashion, textiles, theatre or a related area, it is vitally important that you begin to gather information together as soon as possible so that it can be incorporated into project work.

In your spare time, carry out some of the following:

- At the library, scan newspapers for current fashion and theatre information. Read the fashion and design magazines to familiarize yourself with the work of international designers. Books on costume, textiles, jewellery, sculpture, painting and 3D crafts will all be useful to you.

- Go through old magazines and newspapers for interesting articles about current designers across different areas of design. Look out for unusual drawing techniques used by illustrators and designers and collect cuttings, keeping them in a file for future use.

- Get yourself out and about in the shopping areas nearest to you. Don't just look in shop windows, examine the goods inside. Note prices, the label, craftsmanship and value for money. Ask the sales staff for further information, such as where the goods have been produced.

- Visit art galleries and exhibitions as often as you can.

- If you see interesting fabrics or materials in a store or on a market stall, ask for a sample. Label each swatch with the name of the shop or stall where you found it, details of its composition and of its country of origin, the price per metre width, length and availability in different colourways. Keep a collection of fabric swatches for future reference.

Silhouette shapes

The size and shape of the silhouette is the first thing we notice about a person. It is only as they get closer to us that we start to see details and features. So, when designing we must start with the shape of the body.

You will need drawing materials, A2 paper or drawing pad, tracing or layout paper, magazines, scissors and paints, pastels or other colouring medium. Access to a photocopier for reducing or enlarging images would also be useful.

Silhouette emerging into focus.

Exercise

Select a fashion photograph which features a model in a front-facing pose from a magazine. The model should be wearing a figure-hugging garment or a swimsuit and the pose should have an element of movement about it. Magazines featuring dancers or athletes also provide good images for this project. Your chosen model can be either male or female. If your image is less than A4 top to toe, enlarge it on a photocopier.

Trace round the image, eliminating elaborate hair styles, jewellery, shoes and facial features. Concentrate on obtaining a well-proportioned and athletic-looking silhouette drawn as a continuous outline.

This basic shape can be used as a template. Transfer the tracing on to strong paper or card and then cut out the silhouetted figure, working to the inside of the line so that when it is drawn round the overall image does not become too large or bulky. Alternatively, trace the image through layout paper.

Now reproduce this figure 5 times across an A2 sheet of paper. Alternatively, use photocopies of images reproduced to approximately the same size.

Select one strong colour. Alter the silhouette shapes by applying even and dense colour to make the shapes look:

- Elongated.
- Shorter.
- Top heavy.
- Angular.
- Curvaceous.

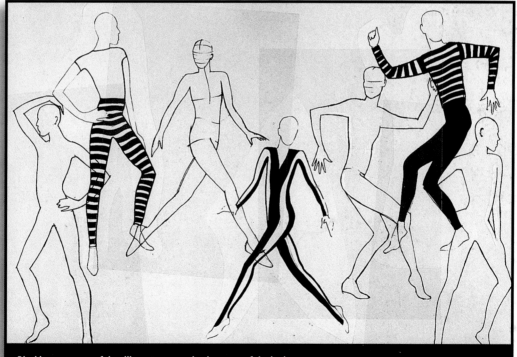

Blocking out parts of the silhouette to emphasize areas of the body.

Exercise

Draw out a set of silhouettes. Using pairs of colours which you consider to contrast in an interesting way, segment the silhouettes into sections which create an appearance of the two colours being evenly balanced.

Repeat this exercise using different silhouette shapes and combinations of colours and extend your use of medium to include pastel, inks, newsprint and even coloured shapes cut from magazines.

Try to capture the look of:

• Top heaviness.
• Bottom heaviness.
• Body muscle or body curves.
• Asymmetric distortion.
• Organic growth.
• Geometry.
• Small patterned shapes.
• Large patterned shapes.

Using texture to contrast the silhouette with its background.

Using the silhouette to experiment with pattern and colour.

Exercise

Imagine that your silhouette shapes are of dancers in a performance, wearing stretch body suits or leotards. You have the task of hand painting them in order to explore the following themes:

• the elements: earth, fire, air and water
• organic forms: leaf, bark, moss, rock, metal, pebbles, seaweed

What distortion and what camouflage can you achieve with your designing?

Finally, draw out, cut and re-mount a set of silhouettes with appropriate backgrounds to give them atmosphere.

Make a handwritten note at the bottom right or left, or beneath each figure, to describe the theme of each silhouette. Keep the notation at the same size and level for each figure and use your natural handwriting. Ambitious lettering only distracts the eye from the artwork. If the silhouettes have been smudged or appear messy then cut them out and re-mount them on to another sheet of paper of the size, colour and quality used for the earlier exercises.

Aim at completing at least 4 x A2 sheets of artwork if you tackle this project. These sheets could provide a good introduction to a portfolio for fashion, theatre, graphics, textiles, jewellery and 3D, or an opening section for a specialist fashion, textile or theatre design portfolio.

Using geometric shapes to dress the silhouette and adding background detail.

The fashion figure

Fashion illustrations convey an overall mood to entice the onlooker to want to know more about a particular outfit. Fashion illustration is similar to life drawing but differs in how it shows the proportions of the body, often presenting a simple but elongated figure.

The method of drawing outlined in the following exercises is a design technique and is not to be confused with observational figure drawing or life drawing. There are many books available which detail all aspects of drawing the fashion figure (see p95).

For this project you will need an either an A2, A3 or A4 sketchbook or pad, a selection of pencils, crayons, paints, pastels and inks, and the assistance of someone who would be willing to pose for you. Alternatively, a full-length or a three-quarter length mirror would enable you to draw yourself.

Exercise

Using a pencil, mark out eight equal sections on a sheet of paper.

The top of the first section will be the top of the head of your model and the bottom section will mark the ankle or heel. Disregard the height, weight or shape of the person.

First, try drawing either yourself or a model within these pre-determined dimensions in a straightforward upright pose. Keep the silhouette slim, as if the figure were almost skeletal. Pay scant attention to the clothes worn by the model at this stage.

Exercise

Fashion designs appear more exciting if they are drawn on a figure that has an exaggerated pose.

Position your chosen model into a standing pose from which they can shift their weight from one leg to the other in an easy and relaxed way. Observe how the shoulders, spine, hips, knees, elbows and ankles all move to accommodate or balance the body so that it remains stable and comfortable.

Now draw a series of five-minute poses indicating the shift of weight distribution from one leg to another. Each pose should show a shift of position.

Block in the balance lines and weight distribution of the body with bold, solid areas of colour. Try to capture the stress and tension of the pose. Use a short piece of crayon or pastel positioned in the hand so that it rests on its side and draw with a sweeping movement in order to capture the line of movement in one gesture.

Each time you follow this exercise, begin by marking in the eight divisions of the body, then add the blocks of colour showing the weight and movement of the pose. Repeat this exercise until it becomes a familiar way of drawing.

Capturing the gesture and action of a pose.

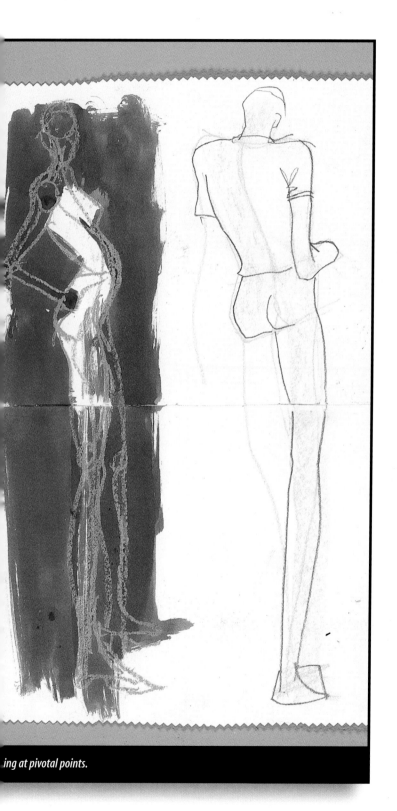

Exercise

Look at the key or pivotal points on the body. These are the spine, shoulders, elbows, wrists, hips, knees and ankles. These points are your frame of reference when drawing the fashion figure and indicate what is happening to the weight distribution on a body.

Use your pencil at arm's length to measure the angles of hip or shoulder tilt and then plot with accuracy the key points of spine, shoulders, hips, knees, elbows, wrists and ankles. Repeat this exercise several more times over the course of 3 or 4 short five-minute poses.

Exercise

Now you are ready to add some detailing. The key to this stage of drawing is in knowing what to look for. On a clothed figure, garment construction lines can indicate just how much tension, twist, or tilt is conveyed in a pose. When drawn accurately, these lines can help convey the gesture or essence of the pose.

Garment construction lines incorporate the following: hairline; hat and scarf positions on head and neck; necklines; shoulder seams; centre front buttons or zip lines; sleeve seams; side seams; bottoms of shirts and sweaters; belts; fly zips; jean seams; skirt and trouser hems and the soles and heels of shoes. It should also be possible at this stage to incorporate pleats, folds and the ribbing of knitwear as these elements are also indicative of body contours which alter with the shift of the pose.

Over a series of 8 or more poses, you can add more and more detailing, building on the pivotal points and key elements of the clothing to convey gradually and more vividly the gesture of the pose.

To complete the image, add body detail such as ears, nose, mouth and hair line, and the position of the hands and feet, including footwear.

Adding in design detail.

Exercise

Trace off 3 images from your fashion figure exercises. Choose a front view; a back view and one part profile and reproduce these images in sets of three. Do this three times for 9 full-length images.

Select a fashion design from a magazine and either trace round it or cut it out and paste it on the drawing sheet close to the first group of your silhouettes.

Copy the details of this design on to your own silhouettes. In each case try to imagine what the design would look like from behind and in profile and alter the existing construction lines to correspond.

On the first set of 3 tracings you might change the length of the sleeves, hems or collars. On the second set of 3 the pockets, buttons or zips. The third set might feature a different cut, style or fit of the garment. In this way you can completely alter the overall shape of the original design.

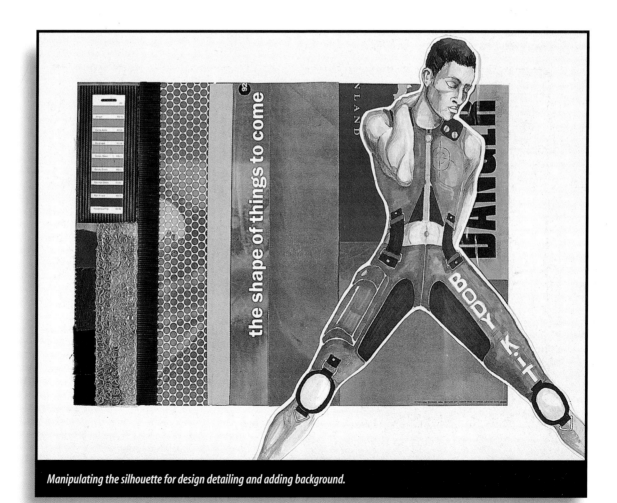

Manipulating the silhouette for design detailing and adding background.

Adding in design detail.

Project

Design a series of simple bodice tops (shirts, waistcoats, T-shirts) to be manufactured in a fabric you have handled and with which you are familiar.

Getting started

Draw out a series of fashion silhouettes, either from the images you traced from magazines or from your fashion figure drawing session. Curtail the figure at below-hip or above-knee level.

Repeat the same image side by side, with a row of back view images below. Alternatively draw the images out in pairs with a front and a back view next to each other. Always draw a front and back view for your designs.

When adding your design drawing to the silhouettes, keep its construction and outline clear and descriptive. Your drawings must communicate with accuracy the detailing, shape, scale and fit of your intended design.

If you want to change the basic body form slightly in order to add some visual interest and variation, alter each drawing with a different facial gesture or hairstyle.

Experiment with texture using different mediums, collage techniques or backgrounds which enhance the visual display or develop the theme of the designs.

The more you work with, read about, look at and handle different materials the more confident you will become in selecting the appropriate fabric for your design.

Remember, these are fashion design drawings, not illustrations.

Developing a theme using simple silhouettes and imagery of landscape, trees and shrubbery.

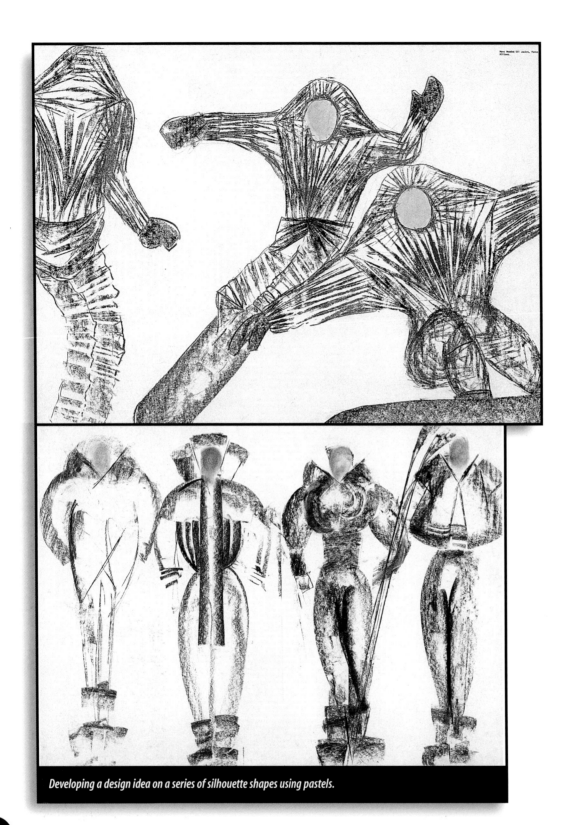

Developing a design idea on a series of silhouette shapes using pastels.

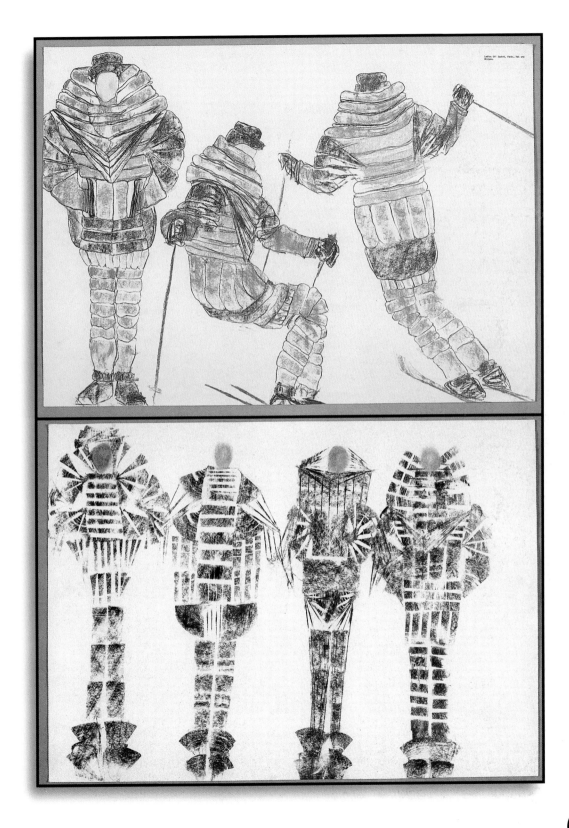

Exercise

Imagine the environment and model that would create the perfect image for your design. Consider how you might construct this scene in a simple but atmospheric way in a fashion illustration.

Use either one or a combination of collage, paint or photographic imagery to construct a background for your design but remember that it should set the scene, not totally dominate it.

Enjoy experimenting with your own individual themes. By doing this you will develop a way of working and a style which is unique to you.

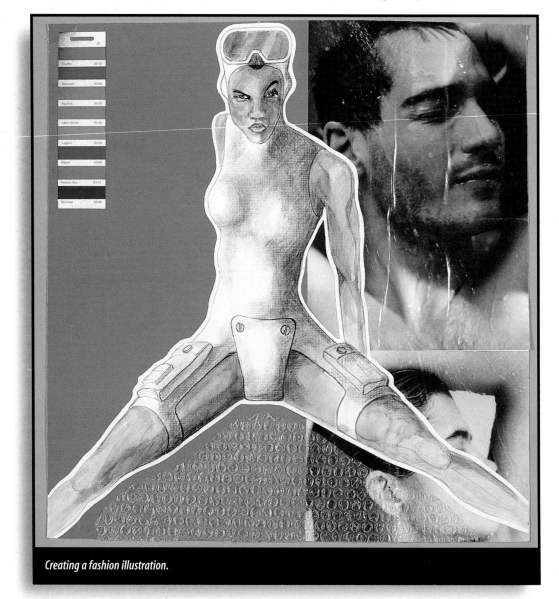

Creating a fashion illustration.

Sketch books, note books and diaries

Sketch book

This is the book where you should record observational drawings of artefacts, objects, people and environments on a daily basis. Drawings in this book could be executed in a matter of seconds or be more sustained. Whether the drawings have been done quickly or slowly, the intention should always be to communicate what has held your interest in the clearest way. The book can be used a source to trigger off and stimulate more developed pieces of work.

Experiment with different drawing techniques. Use soft leaded pencils, pastels, crayons, watercolours, markers, inks, pens and charcoal - anything, in fact, which can be used to register an identifiable mark.

A variety of different-sized drawing books will prove more versatile than one book into which everything is crammed. For example, a larger book can be kept for drawing buildings and for landscape work, whereas a pocket-sized book could travel regularly with you and be used for more unobtrusive drawing on public transport or inside a cafe.

Ideas sketch book.

Visual diary

A visual diary is a daily or weekly recording of your interests and can contain material from exhibition catalogues and magazines, postcards, photographs, travel and cinema tickets, leaves, twigs and even scraps of interesting litter.

Visual journal

A visual journal involves the collection of variously-documented ideas into a magazine format: different sections will feature different themes or topics. However, the journal is not just a vehicle for gathering together items that you find interesting and pasting them down, as in a scrap book. It should be more of an investigative document, clearly indicating your interests and enthusiasms.

Ideas book

An ideas book is intended to be sourced in part by all the other note books and should be kept as a working document for developing ideas. Any final designs from these books can then be transferred on to a larger format on a separate sheet of paper and turned into a presentation visual for inclusion in a portfolio.

Visual diary.

Handwritten notes on the visual note book pages:

Wedding Dress → 1967 BALENCIAGA PARIS ARCHIVES

CABBAGE CAPE 1967 The sheath black evening dress with a 'cabbage cape' of black Gazar – a superb combination of fabric + shape, engulfing the wearer, like a flower or cabbage in its ruffled folds...

LILIUM CANADENSE 1700–1788 Mrs Mary Delany PAPER [MOSAIC] PARIS

flora

in fashion

black + white satin stole/ head-dress

Visual note book.

Visual note book

The visual note book contains material represented with a minimum of words and a maximum use of quick drawing methods. Work with a wide variety of materials and utilize and develop found items as well as sketches. It can be can be any size and need not have a central theme.

Visual note book.

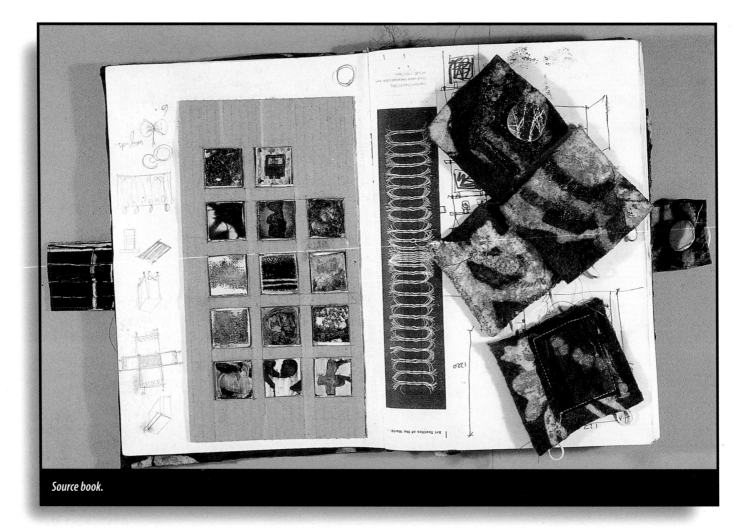

Source book.

Source book

Items in this book are specifically intended to be background or source material which can be fed directly into a particular project or line of enquiry.

The research element of a source book is its strength. Items selected can be analysed for their texture and form, colour, use of line and scale, and also for their historical and cultural influences.

Texture source book.

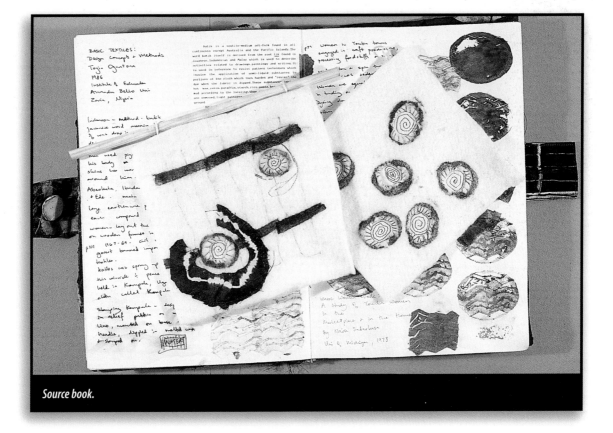

Source book.

Developing research material

A simple but thorough investigation of a topic or theme can really enrich and support a series of designs. The best-researched themes will be clearly seen in the detailing and colour of your final collection.

Research into a topic or idea for designing can be as extensive or as limited as the interests and requirements of the researcher, and is also governed by the time available.

The most common starting points for costume and textile research are nature, landscape, architecture, plants, insects, animals or periods in history – for example, Regency, Victorian, the 1920s, the 1960s. On a much more specific level, individual crafts and skills such as lace making, block printing, quilting and pleating have been studied, analysed and developed into designs.

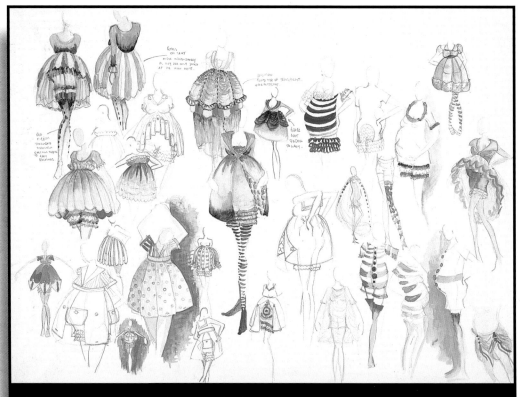

Theme board based on Brighton architecture developed into design sketches and presentation drawings.

Presenting research material

If you intend to present your research work at interview attempt to keep it all to the same standard size. Sort the work into the order in which it was completed and group it into sections which show different aspects of research such as colour, texture, structure or detail.

If you have postcards, photographs, photocopies, or scraps of material which can be collaged together to form an interesting composition this can often produce a very lively and imaginative piece of work.

Design sketches based on the theme of Brighton architecture.

If all your reference material is stored in your source or visual note book but you would still like to mount up a large presentation sheet of ideas this can be done by photocopying details from your drawings and then collaging them together.

Remember that large sheets of mounted work are easier to look at and understand if the areas of detail are clear and uncluttered.

Larger-scale studies of collated research are often referred to as image, source, theme or mood boards. These are used in the design industry as a starting point for generating ideas.

Presentation drawings based on the theme of Brighton architecture.

Theme boards

Themes and ideas are often presented in fashion and textile houses as style boards, mood boards or theme boards.

1960s theme board incorporating collaged magazine images and designs.
Materials: paper, paint and crayon.

Glamour and the movies theme board. Materials: papers, ink, crayon and feathers.

Theme boards, which can vary enormously in size depending on the display panels or wall space available, are a gathering together of fabric swatches, style ideas (sketches or magazine cuttings), colour samples and trimming samples (buttons and braids) and often take the form of a collage which attempts to convey the mood and style of the forthcoming season's collection. These boards set the scene of action for a designer. They are central to creating fresh ideas which will follow a strong theme and be united by an overall look.

In some design rooms the theme board can be found as a collection of drawings, fabrics or man-made objects - such as belts, zips, braids and buttons - loosely gathered together on a spare table. The items can be manipulated like a jigsaw puzzle so that alternative groupings of images, textures and colours can give fresh inspiration to the designer.

You should be able to recognize interesting combinations of patterns, influences and textures and develop these images into a collection of designs.

The following project is designed to help you create your own personal mood board. It is a step-by-step guide of how to go about it. It is very important to go through the listed points carefully. The reasons for this are twofold. It will make you think about specific items which are important to you. By writing them down you have them listed as a permanent reminder ready for use. Secondly, you will be able to identify and eliminate elements which do not interest you.

Project

Present a mounted A1 sheet of images and associated materials which evoke the spirit and atmosphere of fashion for the twenty-first century.

Getting started

This mounted board could be called a mood board, image board or style board.

It is not a scrap book or ideas book given a more glossy presentation, but a serious attempt to analyse what it is about fashion that excites as we approach a new century.

Begin by making a list incorporating some of the following:

- Names of designers whose ideas and ideals are nearest to your own.
- The overall atmosphere you want your images to create eg brilliant colour, hard lines, soft shapes, subtlety.
- Notes on the fashion formats and graphic presentation of fashion features in your favourite magazines.
- The sort of fashion images you like: fun, action, elegant, distorted or natural.
- The types of fabric and textures you like.
- Fashion accessories or images (such as magazine cuttings) that help to harden your ideas.

Now make a more specific list addressing the following points:

- Is the board going to describe colour and images for summer, winter or all seasons?
- Do you want to concentrate on one mood and atmosphere and do you want to include other people's designs as well as your own?
- Do you want to concentrate on women's fashion, men's fashion or childrenswear? Or, alternatively, incorporate several categories on one sheet?
- Do you want to concentrate on one specific theme eg textiles or accessories?

Bearing in mind all the items you have listed, start to gather together some of the following:

- Magazine images which evoke the atmosphere you would like to create.
- Swatches of fabric which suggest themes or ideas.
- Trimmings such as wools, braid buttons, fur, relief, texture and colour reference.
- Colour samples: magazine cuttings, hand-painted fabrics or papers.
- Photocopies of designs which you find interesting both as a contemporary fashion statement and as an indication of future design. Use these photocopies to explain where or on what your ideas are based eg architectural reference, museum collections, nature, digital, movies.

Once you have completed the listings and gathered together the items, begin to work directly on to the board.

Before you paste any item down, alter the composition and groupings of your images and, if necessary, make quick sketches for reference before you try another format. Be inventive with the use of scale and juxtaposition of images.

The size of your board needs to relate to the size of your portfolio and your design work. Your mounting board must be of a substantial board weight, not paper weight. Once fabrics, magazine cuttings, buttons, objects and paint are pasted down, only a firm board will keep them firmly fixed, particularly when the board has to be handled and transported.

It is now time to draw inspiration from these resources and begin the process of developing your ideas into a series of simple fashion designs.

Using the theme of transport to create an elaborate costume.

Using carpet sample boards and applied shapes to generate design ideas.

Experimental body coverings

You can develop your research by constructing a series of experimental body coverings which can later be translated into a set of practical working designs. Creating a body covering from unusual materials allows you to look at existing sources in an innovative way, giving you the freedom to experiment with scale, texture, colour and form as a starting point for developing ideas into other art and design areas.

Almost any topic of interest that has some visual content can be used as a source of study for this initial research period.

Visual research

Research your chosen source, theme or idea through drawing, painting, collage with photocopies, photographs, relief work on paper using other materials and maquette making. This is essential to identifying and understanding more fully the essential shapes, forms, structure and colour of your theme (see pp36-7).

Next, develop your work into three dimensions. This should be a natural progression from the collage work begun during the initial research period. It is relief work, maquette building and textural work, all still based on the original research drawings but perhaps abstracted, altered or distorted in scale.

Materials and equipment

Only go out and search for materials after the initial research period. Your research will dictate the type of materials which will be required. Obviously, if the materials - such as card, paper or newsprint - have been pre-set as part of the project, then work with these directly in three dimensions on the body.

The emphasis of these projects is to invent, re-interpret and re-define using unusual and untried materials. Do not over-use ready-made items as they can restrict innovation and should be kept for essential detail only.

- Scissors.
- Craft knives and cutting mat.
- Steel ruler.
- Measuring tape.
- Adhesive tape (including double-sided and masking).
- Adhesives (all purpose).

- Stapler.
- Paper clips.
- Dressmaking pins.
- Blue-tac.
- Leather punch.
- Eyelet pliers.
- Rubber bands.
- Paints and brushes.
- Pencils, pastels or similar.
- P.V.A. medium.
- Marker pens.
- Glitter pens.
- Coloured inks.
- Spray fix (necessary if using pastels or chalk).
- Papers and boards of all weights, colours and textures.
- Discarded packaging.
- Films and foils.
- Strings, cottons, wools.
- Wire.
- Any haberdashery or hardware item that could be used as a temporary or permanent fixing method.

Body coverings based on a study of armour.
Materials: from paper and wire to foam and industrial waste products.

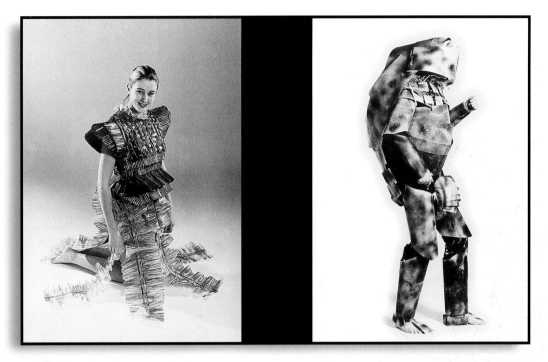

Getting started

You can begin working with your chosen materials directly on to a dress stand, building the body covering section by section.

Another method is to spend time working with body silhouettes outlined on paper. You can transfer shapes onto the silhouettes, experimenting with the textures and materials you have selected. Such pre-planning can eliminate unworkable elements, streamline over-elaborate ideas and help to identify a starting point.

Two-dimensional plans can change dramatically when body coverings are constructed in full-scale. You must be prepared to be flexible when your pre-planned ideas are found to be unmanageable or visually cluttered.

- Go for bold, overall impact and clearly-defined shapes.
- Allow enough flexibility for body movement.
- At regular intervals stand back from and walk round the structure, assessing it from all angles.
- Be prepared to change any section which does not balance or help towards the total effect.
- Have only one or two focal points (areas of high detail) or strong colours which stand out from the rest of the piece, otherwise the overall effect will be one of confusion and clutter.
- Keep referring back to your original research. Try to encapsulate as much of the excitement and interest of your early observations in the final body covering.
- Towards the final stages - particularly when adding surface decoration or pattern - assess the overall impact by standing back and viewing the body covering as if through the viewfinder of a camera.
- If you are building your structure directly onto the stand without referring to preliminary silhouette drawings, document each stage of development by making simple sketches. This record will be of great value should you lose direction and need to return to an earlier stage of construction.

Body covering based on the work of Antonio Gaudi.

Project

Make a study of armour from any period in history and from any country in the world. Devise a full-size body covering out of paper and card which embodies the most interesting aspects of your research (see pp44-5).

Project

Devise a full-size experimental body covering based on your personal interpretation of the work of a designer, craftsperson, painter or sculptor. Beware of creating a too literal translation; make an attempt to capture the 'essence' of the work (see p46).

Project

Using newsprint or magazines together with one other contrast material, construct a full-size body covering. The result should reflect the most interesting aspects of your materials: colour printing, typography, glossy covers (see p48).

Body covering exploiting metallic surfaces.

Project

Using images of natural objects such as
plants, birds, fish, coral as your source for
research, create a full-length experimental
body covering, incorporating a variety of
flexible materials of both natural and man-
made origin (see p49).

Project

Go out into the streets or, alternatively, to
a place of particular interest and make a
series of studies – drawings, paintings
and/or photographs – of the local
architecture and architectural detail.
Develop your research into a full-scale
body covering. Try to retain some of the
most interesting aspects of your drawings
and the atmosphere of the original source
material (see p50).

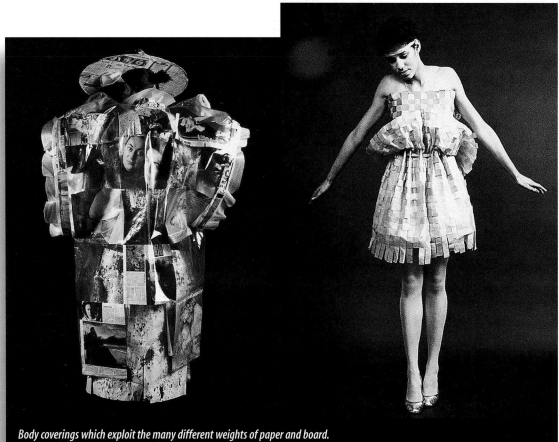

Body coverings which exploit the many different weights of paper and board.

Body coverings based on natural forms.

49

Body covering based on a study of a local area (Holborn by night).

From experimental work to practical solutions

Developing your experimental work into more practical solutions allows you to demonstrate your ability not only as a creative thinker but also as a practical designer.

However, interesting ideas which stop at the very experimental stage and are simply presented as research topics or themes can sometimes be sufficient for an interview. Often it is the wildly experimental work that indicates to a course interviewer whether or not you have an individual and creative way of thinking.

From the exercise in the previous chapter you should have a finished piece of experimental work, either in the form of a total or part of a body covering. You should also have taken photographs of the body covering being worn.

You will need a large space in which to spread out all the work generated by and collected for the last project, including drawings, photographs, materials, samples of experimental textiles and surface treatments and, of course, the body covering itself.

The next step is to dismantle the costume!

Retain the sections which you find most interesting, perhaps because of their colour, texture or detailing. Re-mount these sections, or at least part of them, on to separate sheets of card or paper.

Take five tracings from the photograph of the final costume being worn, including the figure, as a silhouette outline. On the first silhouette trace off the horizontal lines, on the second, the vertical lines, and on the third, the different sections that make up the body covering.

Having spent time looking at the different textures, colours and shapes from the dismantled sections, transfer them to the remaining two silhouettes, choosing those elements which are individually most eye catching or which, when collaged together, look most dynamic.

Ask yourself:

• Does the texture or colour balance across the silhouette, or does one section dominate?
• Is the image interesting?

The next step is to decide on an area or category of design for which you could produce a range of garments, textile ideas, jewellery or accessory designs.

Try to avoid the obvious. For example, if you have been researching the seashore, the collection of designs you produce need not be swimwear or resortwear. Similarly, surfaces which shine need not necessarily be developed into glitzy eveningwear or heavily-textured surfaces into weave or knits. It is more important to attempt to design within an area that holds your interest and enthusiasm.

Categories of design include:

• Outerwear, which can be subdivided into coats, suits and separates for town, country, formalwear, workwear or casualwear.
• Daywear: separates, casual, smart, special occasion or formal, leisurewear or sportswear.
• Sportswear: either performance wear or the more casual variety.
• Eveningwear: formal eveningwear or evening separates.
• Lingerie.
• Maternity clothes.
• Childrenswear.
• Specialist clothing: performance sportswear, performance workwear, medical necessities, even prosthetics.
• Theatre costume, fancy dress and carnival.

• Accessories: millinery, footwear, belts, bags, luggage - each can command a collection in its own right.
• Jewellery: precious metalwork or costume jewellery.

In all of the above categories you can design for either a male or female, or for both if you think that this is appropriate.

When you are ready to begin, draw the fashion silhouette that will suit your chosen design category (see pp13-22). For example, if you are intending to design sportswear then choose a silhouette that has some action about it and, if possible, indicates the sport for which the designs are intended. If your designs are to feature a more formal look, then select a more sophisticated pose.

Transfer the dominant lines or textures from your traced images on to the silhouettes, then detail sections of texture and colour to emphasize or flatter the contours of the body.

Use this simple method to transfer shape, texture, line, structure and colour from your research into design ideas. When you have exhausted one area of your research either change the design category or look at another area of your experimental work.

Eveningwear and women's daywear are the most popular categories, so think about designing within an area that is more unusual such as childrenswear, sportswear or accessories. This means your portfolio presentation work will be different from the rest and be more likely to be noticed and remembered.

Projects and themes

The following lists contain suggestions to clarify your thoughts and generate design ideas. Use them as a frame of reference. Investigate the themes through drawing, photography and colour analysis, simulating textures and looking at the historical influences. Each theme should stimulate a set of drawings, texture boards and research boards which can then be developed into experimental or practical proposals. Any interest or hobby can be used as a basis for research and therefore as a topic for a theme.

After choosing a theme or project, work through the instructions for theme boards (pp34–40) or body coverings (pp42–50).

Themes

- Nature.
- Animals, butterflies, insects, birds, prehistoric animals, flora and fauna.
- Natural phenomena and geology.
- Earth, wind, fire, water.
- Seasons.
- Weather conditions.
- Areas of the world - arctic, tropics, desert.
- Cultures - Third World, tribal, rituals, religion.
- Signs of the Zodiac.
- Architecture.
- Materials.
- Typography, magazine graphics.
- Periods in history.
- The work of a painter/sculptor/craftsperson.
- Technology.
- Sport.
- Manufacturing and craft techniques: pleating, ruching, tucking, lace, embroidery, weaving.

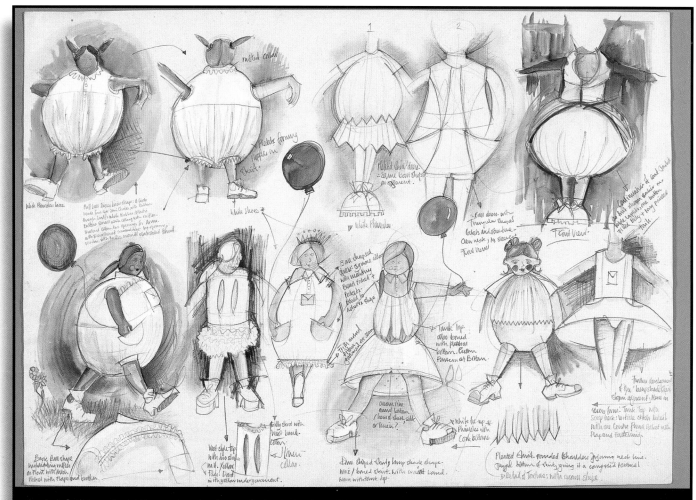

Developing designs of a child's party dress (see 'Personal collection' project, p57).

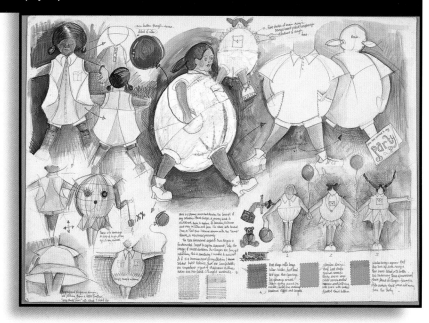

Project

Design an extravagantly luxurious garment for full-scale manufacture using the cheapest possible fabric you can find. In other words, 'fake' your original idea by employing as many materials and methods of improvisation as you can.

Project

An enterprising glossy magazine features a regular monthly article about young designers. Those selected for promotion are thought to be showing remarkable talent in their chosen sphere. You have been invited by the Fashion and Features editors of this periodical to present a short profile of yourself, which is to include a series of personal designs.

Produce a collection of four designs which you would like to see manufactured and offered for sale bearing your own name or trade label. It could be for a particular store, chain of outlets, an individual shop or a mail order catalogue. Your presentation work should fit into a standard folder of A2, A3 or A4 size and should be presented as loose pages. In this way it can be viewed page by page as a book or as an exhibition mounted on a display system.

Getting started

A good profile should not only include your name, age, possibly a photograph and the above design work, but any information you consider relevant such as previous industrial or educational training prior to your chosen career. You could also include information about your interests, activities and travel.

Your designs could be presented as illustrations, coupled with more detailed working drawings or, alternatively, as a straightforward set of clear design drawings. You should include sample swatches of materials for your designs whenever possible.

Project

Shop study: Select an area in your nearest town or city which is considered to have an above average quota of 'fashionable' shops or stores.

- List the shops and their location.
- Categorize the shops – individual shop, chain, department store, craft market etc.
- Elaborating on each selected category analyse the following:
  - the target market of the shop.
  - the interior: who designed it? How does the decor, style etc emphasize this type of retail outlet?
  - designers stocked and their nationality.
  - prices: select individual items or an overall price category.
  - individual comments and any additional information you would like to add (ask a member of staff if necessary).

On completing your listings, select one shop which you feel could successfully stock a range of your designs. Produce a small collection of designs with this particular retail outlet in mind.

Present your information and designs in a small hard backed folder or as a series of sheets of paper clipped together. Your information need not be typed but should be neat and legible.

Research board and designs for outerwear exploring unusual methods of folding, wrapping and pleating.

Project

Personal collection
Design a collection of garments or accessories which will bear your own name. It could be a Spring/Summer collection, or an Autumn/Winter collection. Choose one of the categories below and design for men, women, children or any combination of these.

- Outerwear: coats, suit jackets, trousers, rainwear.
- Dresses: daywear, officewear for any season.
- Separates: combinations of shirts, blouses, trousers, skirts.
- Late afternoon or special occasion wear: more expensive, better fabrics, more detailing, not too functional.
- 'After six': cocktail wear for semi-formal occasions, linking with special occasion wear.
- Eveningwear: informal or formal.
- Lingerie or contour design.
- Childrenswear.
- Resortwear: passive sportswear and leisurewear.
- Active sportswear: performance clothes.
- Maternity.
- Knitwear (this can be included in all the above categories but also used as a complete collection in itself).
- Accessories (as collections in their own right, or as part of any of the previous categories).

Getting started

A collection should be at least six complete outfits which have a unifying theme either in their design, shape, colour or fabric choice.

Begin by producing a series of rough ideas.

Try to build upon or extend one or two ideas or themes such as an interesting overall body silhouette or a clever design detail. After making roughs, re-select and re-draw the designs which you feel are the strongest in the group. Your final presentation drawings should be clear in their design detail and show all construction lines. Each set of designs should be accompanied by fabric/material swatches.

Project

Travel wardrobe for a 4-day business trip
Design and compile a travel wardrobe for a 4-day business trip. The wardrobe can be for either a man or woman and the designs need to cover the following items:

- Travel clothing.
- Conference/business wear.
- Casualwear.
- Eveningwear.
- Luggage.
- Hand luggage.
- Accessories.

The itinerary for our traveller is itemized below.

Day 1
Travel: by train - airline - taxi.
Evening: conference registration followed by buffet dinner.

Day 2
Conference.
Evening: night out with business associates - dinner and night club.

Day 3
Conference.
Evening: cocktail reception followed by a formal end-of-conference dinner.

Day 4
Morning: sightseeing tour .
Return travel home: taxi - airline - train.

T-shirt designs (see 'T-shirt' project, p59)

The choice of location for the conference and the home of the traveller is up to you. The wardrobe will need to be appropriate for the venue, the season and climate and for both the business and after-conference element of the trip.

Present your designs as a fully-accessorized collection, using the appropriate day and venue as a title for each set of design drawings or illustrations. Incorporate fabric swatches wherever possible.

Refer to the personal collection notes on p57 if you need help getting started.

Project

Make a short study of any one (or, at most, two which are closely linked) of the following processes and develop your research notes into a small collection of fashion ideas. Present your ideas as a series of finished design drawings.

- Draping.
- Pleating (include tucks and ruching).
- Smocking (include gathering).
- Quilting.
- Boning.
- French seaming.
- Top stitching.
- Machine knitting.
- Hand knitting.

Develop these design drawings into fashion illustrations. Alternatively, make up a section of one of your designs from the collection. Try the following design details:

- An embroidery sample taken from one of your designs.
- A pocket sample.
- A cuff detail.
- A fabric print, knit or weave sample.

Project
T-shirt
Trace the origins of the T-shirt. Compile a short research notebook, fact file or mood board showing its development, particularly during recent decades. Display your facts and visuals in a lively and interesting format.

Using methods and processes suitable for stretch cotton fabric, develop a personalized or customized T-shirt.

Getting started
Bear in mind the following useful technical information:

- Fabric paints and dyes should be fixed if the garment is to be washed.
- Hand painting, screening and spraying should be done when the fibre is slightly stretched and with a board slotted between the back and front sections to keep them apart.
- Read the instructions on the tin of dye before attempting dip dye, tie dye or an overall colourfast technique.
- Sew cotton fabric on a machine using a ball point needle which prevents holes and laddering on stretch fabric. Use zig-zag stitch where possible.
- Any padding or quilting techniques should make use of a polyester or washable wadding.
- Studs, rivets, eyelets, zips and buttons should be applied after reinforcing the material with a fusible interfacing.
- It may be necessary to support your T-shirt with a stretch fusible backing material before you begin any appliqué or beading work.

Project

Historical costume

Select a traditional costume or item of clothing, either because the culture is one with which you are familiar or because you find the item has interesting qualities such as shape, structure, colour or texture.

Study all aspects of this garment. Through simple, annotated sketches, trace its development from its historical source through to the present day.

Suggested items for research:

- Leather jacket.
- Swimming costume.
- Football strip.
- Rugby shirt.
- Pullover and cardigan.
- Suit.
- Uniforms of all varieties.
- Theatre or performance clothing: Pierrot Harlequin, Clown or Jester.
- Ballet or dance costumes: tutu, carnival costume.
- Waistcoat.
- Kimono.
- Trousers.
- An item of underwear.
- A particular type of boot, shoe or slipper.
- Dirndl skirt.
- Smock.
- Christening gown.
- Party dress.
- Wedding dress.

Compile a short notebook of photocopies, annotated drawings and magazine cuttings to illustrate your research.

Try to find examples of designers from any field and from any era who have used similar historical and traditional sources for their designs.

Using all the information you have gathered, design a small collection of garments suitable for either Spring/Summer or Autumn/Winter. This collection, whilst being exciting and innovative, should retain some of the most enduring features of your original research.

Project

Instant couture

Select any weight of calico or plain material in a 2 or 3 metre length. Contrast this with a short length of felt. Using scissors and an all-purpose or craft adhesive, cut and construct a garment directly on to a dressmaking stand. Do not use traditional methods of pattern cutting and do not plan by drawing the design beforehand. Allow the three-dimensional form to develop slowly, stage by stage, without having any finished design idea in your mind before you begin.

The felt should be used to emphasize a detail or form a contrast section. Alternatively, it could be used to form an embellishment to complete the outfit.

This project needs no dressmaking skills, just access to a dressmaking stand and some basic materials. It can be repeated using different coloured felts for a series of instant cut and stick garments. These can then be photographed on the stand or modelled and fully accessorized to give a substantial 3-D project for a section in a portfolio.

Project

Stand out from the crowd
Design a garment to be worn under
special lighting installed at a new and very
innovative night club.

Getting started

Make a study of different lighting effects
and the way in which they affect certain
materials and colours. Include photography
in your research.

Present your final designs accompanied by
samples of materials and, if possible,
illustrate the garment being worn under
the lighting for which it was designed.

Project

A hat for all seasons
Design and make a head covering that
fulfils the following conditions:

• It is able to combat likely weather conditions.
• It is comfortable to the wearer.
• It displays an interesting structure and inventive uses
  of unusual materials.
• It is simple enough in design either to be fully made
  up by the designer or to be mocked-up in three
  dimensions using substitute materials.

Getting started

Visit the library to investigate past or
current fashion magazines and design and
sports journals. Look at books on historical
costume, theatre costume and at any
information on past or current millinery.

Visit camping, expedition and nautical
clothing and equipment shops in order to
look at current designs and the materials
that have been used.

Make notes and sketches for reference. If
possible, take photographs of any
interesting headgear you see around you.

Make preliminary drawings and collect
photocopies of images you find
stimulating. Develop your research into a
design proposal as demonstrated in the
previous chapters (pp41-50, 51-2). Do not
over-plan your ideas on paper but branch
out into model making as soon as you can.

Mock-up the final design by substituting
cheaper and readily-available materials.

Discarded packaging, papers and cards,
polythene and film can produce a very
substantial and realistic interpretation of an
original design in a very short space of
time. When working in this way adopt
immediate ways of assembling materials -
gluing, lacing, eye-letting - rather than
time-consuming methods such as machine
and hand stitching.

Keep a photographic record of everything
you make. On completion, photograph it
in its appropriate weather condition as
well as in a studio or other more
controlled setting.

Make sure that the notes accompanying
the project are kept brief and easy to
understand.

Project

Historic research
Research the history of patchwork, once
simply a means of extending the life of a
garment or artefact, but which, more
recently, has been used for creative effect.

Body coverings from recycled materials (see 'Historic research' project, p61).

Re-cycle or re-construct any one or a combination of the following into a small collection of garments, artefacts or accessories.

- Old knitwear - all types, all yarns, all colours.
- Old tailored suits - all types.
- Old ties.
- Empty polyethylene bottles.
- Plastic or paper bags.
- Flexible packaging nets or film.

Refer to pp31-40 and pp41-50 for methods of research and to pp51-2 for suggestions in transferring research material through to design ideas.

Project

Supporter of the year
You are your team's most outrageous supporter. You are always spotted by the cameras and the press wearing the team colours. Design yourself a new image for the next international sporting event. You will be part of a large-capacity crowd - do not let the cameras pass you by!

Getting started

Research the relevant sports kit and memorabilia. Then either re-design the entire club image, offering fresh ideas for both the sporting kit and club souvenirs, or, after finishing your research, use the visual material you have collected to design yourself an outrageous and eye-catching outfit.

Develop your ideas through to design drawings as outlined on pp51-2. As a final illustration you could enlarge a crowd scene and place the final design in a suitable position, as if on camera.

This project would benefit from having theme and/or visual research boards as a starting point.

Project

Corporate identity
Make a series of drawings of mechanical objects or pieces of machinery, and using these as a starting point, design a range of functional practical garments for the daywear of light industrial or computer/technical workers. The large, progressive company for whom they work wishes to provide its employees not with a uniform but with a style reference and image which reflects the status of that company in the world of commerce.

Present a set of design drawings accompanied by material swatches. If possible, extend these drawings into a final illustration by using a photocopied enlargement of an appropriate workplace, featuring a selection of your final designs positioned within the work environment on figures reduced to scale.

Project

Body game
Devise a series of individual shapes which can be joined together to form a structure on the body and then taken apart and reassembled in a different way so as to fit either the same or a different part of the body. This body kit will have adaptability, flexibility and incorporate ingenious methods of linking the separate pieces.

Getting started

Draw out basic geometric shapes and overlap them to form a continuous web or blanket. Try to mix shapes of differing sizes. Incorporate interesting textures and a variety of colours. Transfer your ideas on to a silhouette of the body in order to be able to experiment with scale.

Visit haberdashery departments for conventional methods of joining materials and craft and hardware stores for more unusual methods: wires, chain and hooks.

When you have chosen the best materials for the job, make up one small section as a sample. If you have time, make up the kit.

Keep a photographic record of each step of the model making process and photograph the final results.

For a children's alternative to this project see pp76-7.

Project

Olympic sportswear 1
Design a collection of sportswear for the next Summer or Winter Olympic Games. Take a good look at the existing sportswear on the market and document your findings using photocopies, drawings, brochure and magazine cuttings as a series of small but themed visual research boards.

Olympic sportswear 2
Design the opening parade outfit for one nationality. Also design the team track suit which will be worn by both male and female athletes. The final design should embody the vitality and spirit of the nation it represents.

Getting started
These projects can be worked together or tackled as separate design briefs.

The first project asks you to present your research as a series of boards. Themed boards can also be used to supply background information for project two.

Use a body silhouette that has an athletic image so that the presentation drawings for your final designs have an energetic feel.

Project

Nature study
Make a study of a garden or of formal landscape gardening in general, observing the layout and arrangement of:

• Flower beds, hedges, lawns.
• Architectural features: paths. walls, fountains.
• The organization of small gardens, herb, vegetable, secret gardens.

Collect reference material, making notes and drawings of interesting aspects.

Extend your study to include a large still-life of plants and flowers which you can set up and leave unchanged for several days. From this arrangement produce a set of drawings, including colour studies, using paint, pastels and collage, as well as detailed drawings employing both line and tone.

Finally, review all the research and work generated from the still life and, using this as source material, begin ideas for designs in any of the following areas:

• Textiles: wall hangings, cushions, bedspreads, tiles or surface decorations.
• Body coverings.
• Fashion accessories: millinery, jewellery, shoes.
• Interior decoration: surface decoration for walls, floors, lighting and furniture.

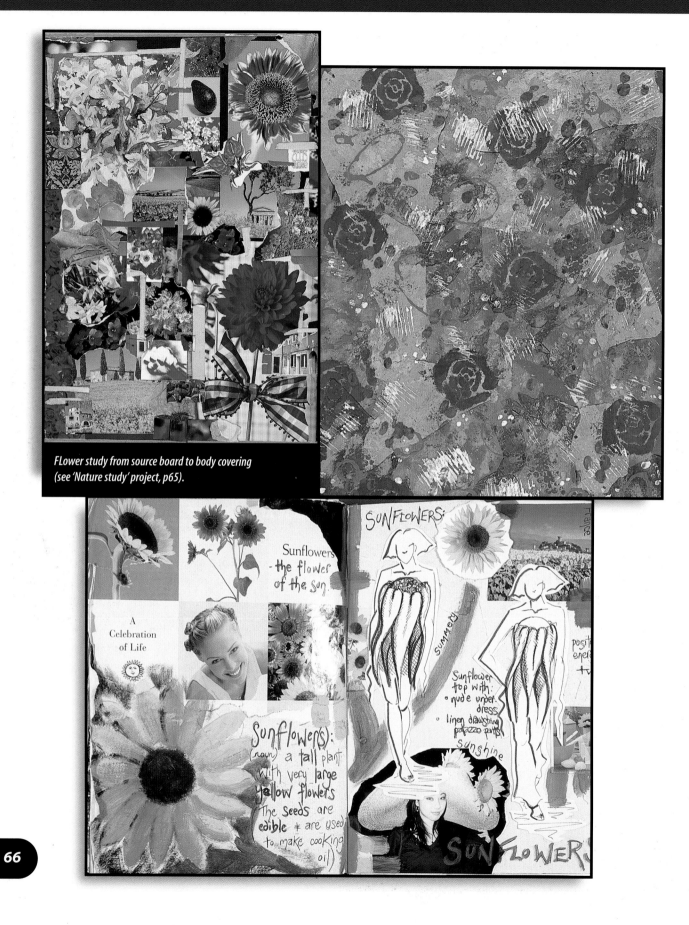

FLower study from source board to body covering
(see 'Nature study' project, p65).

Experimental costumes based on shapes taken from drawings of machinery and early aircraft (see 'Mechanical drawing' project, p69).

Project

Architectural drawing
Make a series of drawings using architecture as your source of information. Expand these into detailed sketches concentrating on elements which you find particularly interesting and then work on them further by means of collage and model making.

Using this material, develop a series of practical designs for a simple garment,

accessory or set of interchangeable separates which should retain the spirit of your original research.

If you need help with the transfer of research into design ideas then refer back to previous chapters (pp41-50, 51-2) and re-read the relevant sections on other more detailed projects.

Project

Mechanical drawing

Make a series of drawings of mechanical objects or pieces of machinery. Using these drawings as a reference for shape and scale, devise and make a flexible structure to cover either the entire body or, alternatively, to become a highly-detailed and ingenious piece of body adornment.

Follow the method of working as for the architecture project and use the guidelines outlined in the chapters on body coverings and developing experimental work into practical solutions for help on how to transfer line, texture, form and colour into design work.

Project

Corporate identity 2

Design a full set of outfits for all the staff and crew of a newly-launched airline, ferry or rail company. Your task is to identify the full range of outfits required and to project the ambition of a forward-thinking company. The style should be distinctive but comfortable to work in. The designs can be for summer or winter and as this collection would be classified as workwear, priority ought to be given to durable and easy care fabrics.

Getting started

Visit an airport, travel terminal or station in order to observe all the different personnel. Make detailed drawings and take photographs as this will help you to identify the different tasks involved within the company and capture the atmosphere of the working environment.

Alternatively, or in support of the information gathered on the visit, search through travel magazines for relevant material.

When your research is concluded, follow the outlines given for theme boards and experimental costumes to help you develop your research into design ideas. In addition to a set of clear design drawings try to produce at least one final illustration as part of your presentation. Wherever possible, include sample swatches of the type of material you might use and offer different groups of colours ('colour stories') for the uniforms.

Project

Words into image

Expand any of the following words into a set of design ideas for costume and/or accessories:

- Camouflage.
- Reflection.
- Sound.
- Dazzle.
- Glow.
- Illusion.
- Distortion.
- Shine.

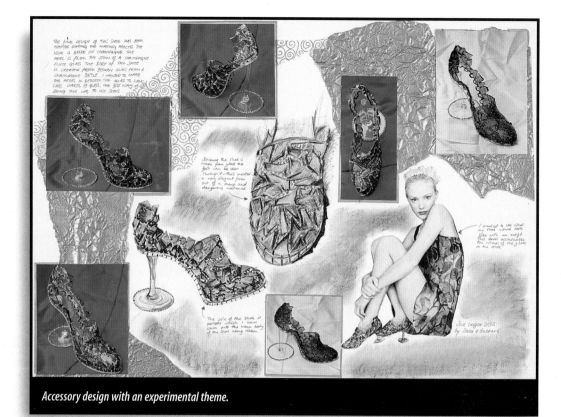

Accessory design with an experimental theme.

Getting started

Begin by drawing and listing the images or associations that each or a selection of the above words has for you. Try to select words that conjure up fresh, unusual and innovative ideas.

Seek out unlikely sources for materials. Use the library to discover unusual information such as different forms of camouflage in the animal and insect kingdom, or the ways in which artists have represented reflection.

Use photography, magazine images, drawings, photocopies etc. as a source of reference.

Look back over pp41–50 for ideas and methods of working.

Present your final drawings, illustrations, mock ups and photographs in such a way that even the presentation reflects and enhances the chosen word.

Project

Technical

Design a simple structure which is capable of doing the following:

- Being worn as a simple garment or harness over the top of everyday clothing.
- Holding everyday equipment necessary for a designer whilst working at a table or drawing board.
- Being adapted to a holdall.

• Able to be used as an independent structure to support tools and equipment if left suspended on a studio stool, chair or hook.

Getting started

Consider all the human factors involved in this project.

Compile research notes which take into account work clothes, multi-pocketed bags and tool kits currently on the market.

Make full use of easy means of assembly, fixings, strapping and reinforcing methods. Look for strong, washable materials which might be of use to include as sample swatches on your design sheets.

This is an ideal project for displaying your three-dimensional skills without having to cope with laborious sewing techniques. Small sections can be produced as samples to accompany your final designs.

On concluding your research follow the guidelines given in pp41-50 and pp51-2 for help in transferring visual reference into three-dimensional studies.

Project

Body game

Design a game that can be played by several people. The main device for the game has to be the structure of the clothing, harness or items worn which you

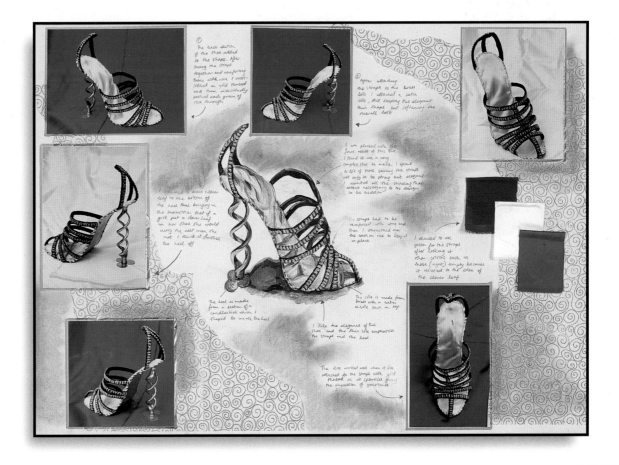

Carnival costume (see 'Tropical paradise' project, p73).

Refer to p53 for the method of working and to pp41-50 and pp51-2 for help in transferring research into design concepts.

Project

Tropical paradise

Design and make an elaborate costume and head-dress to be worn at a street carnival. The theme of the carnival is 'Tropical Paradise'. Make thorough notes, drawings and photographs, researching your subject by visiting the library, tropical hothouse gardens, bird and animal sanctuaries and greengrocers with a wide selection of exotic fruit.

Refer to pp41-50 and pp51-2 for research methods and help in transferring ideas into design work.

Project

Child's play

Design a jump-suit suitable for adventurous activity in an outdoor playground. This is intended as an alternative to the child's own clothes and needs to be capable of withstanding the reckless pursuits of a 5-7 year old!

Getting started

Compile a set of drawings of children at play. Record the type of play equipment they are likely to encounter in a supervised play park and the types of play clothing that already exist on the market.

have designed and which are essential for the playing of the game.

Getting started

Make reference to the human scale at all times in your sketch work

Compile a series of studies of existing games or use historical reference to source your ideas.

Refer to pp41-50 and pp51-2 and the projects in this chapter for ideas on methods of working and presentation.

Don't forget to make the clothing light, tough and adjustable. A two-year

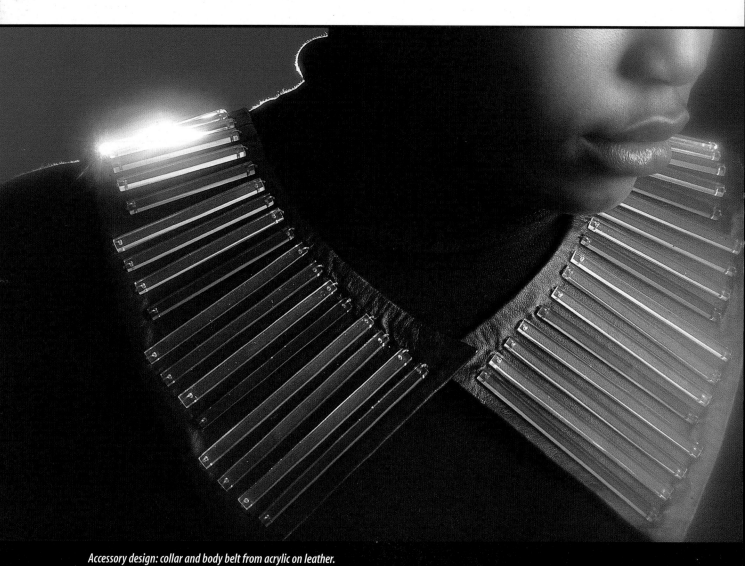

Accessory design: collar and body belt from acrylic on leather.

difference in a child's age can mean a substantial variation in size.

Produce full working drawings and sample swatches of suitable materials.

Project

Child's play 2

Design a series of interlocking modules or units that could be used by children in the following ways:

• As a snap together kit for wearing on the body.
• As a linking or snap together blanket for tent making, or for use as a mattress or hammock.

Produce full working drawings, including details of the joining and linking methods used, plus sample swatches and manufacturing notes. If possible make up a series of your proposed units to scale.

Don't forget to use your drawing and photographic studies of children in your final illustrations and try to show the final design actually being used by the children.

Inflatable bubble blocks by Nancy Ewers (see 'Child's play 2' project, p76).

Experimental costumes based on a study of architecture (see 'Architectural drawing' project, p68).

Experimental costumes using recycled materials (see 'Historic research' project, p61).

Reviewing your work

The following chapter seeks to help you to review the completed work from the previous chapters so that the best or most thorough projects can show your versatility and strengths.

You will need to be demanding and honest with yourself during this review stage. If possible, it would be advisable to gain a second opinion on your work from someone with more experience.

In order to review your work, each section needs to be sorted into the order it was completed and kept in separate piles.

Apply this simple check list of questions to each different topic, exercise or project.

• Does the finished work to date show variety?
• Is the scale of work in each project varied?
• Are the details highlighted in your work clear?
• Have you used colour in each project?
• Is there too much or too little colour?
• Have you included textures, fabrics or other material samples?
• Does the presentation work look as if it has been produced to your best standard?
• Are there sections with which you are not happy and need to re-do or re-work? If so, which ones and how?

The answers will help you to identify what needs to be done and put right simple things you may have overlooked.

By looking at all the work you will be able to assess how much needs to be done before it is ready to be mounted for the portfolio.

If the projects you have reviewed appear too similar then re-read the chapters on body coverings, theme boards and themes and attempt a project that is totally different. Allow a short working time and use different methods of researching and recording your observations.

For example, if all of the previous projects have involved lots of drawing for research, this time use photographs and collages of textured materials. Or, if the earlier work has a great deal of bright colour then select a more subtle palette or, alternatively, work in monochrome only using whites through to greys and black. If previously you have relied on pattern or elaborate detail, then on the new work use plain or textured surfaces on simplified shapes.

Be prepared to take risks and do not slip back into the familiar techniques that have proved comfortable and have been easily achieved the past.

Organizing your portfolio

A well-thought out and clearly-presented portfolio is not only good to look at but communicates a great deal about you as a designer. Organizing your portfolio should not be rushed. If your work is innovative and the concepts exciting, the presentation needs to show these qualities clearly.

It has long been the practice to mount a general art portfolio to A1 size. Although this is big, it does mean that all large-scale drawings can be included with just a trim and a clean up.

Design work and presentation drawings are usually worked on A2, A3 or even A4 paper and, for professional presentations, are mounted in the appropriate-sized portfolio or display case. However, if you have a mixture of large A1 size artwork and smaller design work and already possess an A1 portfolio it might be better to combine the two types of work in the larger case.

For the purposes of this chapter we will assume all work to be of A2 size or smaller with all mounts the same size.

Most interviewers will be prepared to look at two fairly compact and well-presented portfolios but would probably prefer only one. It is also worth remembering that if you are carrying notebooks, research projects and some 3-D work too bulky to fit into a portfolio case, two portfolios could be almost impossible to manage on public transport.

The choice is yours and largely depends on the size of your pocket, how much you can carry with ease and the type of work you are presenting.

Initial selection

It should be relatively easy to go through you work and discard that which you feel falls way below your best standard. Try to get a second opinion from someone you trust before you begin the selection and after you have completed it.

Choose what you would consider to be your very finest pieces of work, to a maximum of 30 sheets, and place them on one side.

Sort through the remaining work and on a separate pile place the second best 30 sheets.

Set the rest on a third pile but do not discard anything.

If there are items in the third pile which are not wholly satisfactory but contain an interesting sketch or section, place these into a reserve pile. These images could be useful at a later stage for incorporating into another presentation or for inclusion in sketch or research books.

It is likely that the OUT pile will outweigh the IN, but at this stage it is very important not to throw work away as anything that is good should be used. It is much better to present 20-30 sheets of the very best work than 50 mounts which include a lot of middling quality.

Portfolio cases

Most portfolio display cases are of a standard type and can be obtained from specialist art equipment shops and also at selected branches of well-known stationers. A display portfolio has a zipped outer case and a central spine of spring clips which holds transparent sleeves in position. The sleeves are designed to take two sides of artwork and often eliminate the need to mount up work on stiff card as they support and protect the work within the case.

Before deciding on which work to mount and how to position it, it is necessary to know whether it will fit into clear display sleeves or have to be mounted separately on board and placed as loose leaves in the portfolio.

Always check the number of sleeves the case is designed to hold. Some have wide spines and clips and can take a substantial amount of work. Others are intended to take a limited number of sleeves and for this reason could prove unsuitable. The transparent display sleeves can be bought separately and added as extras to the folder but do not cram the case because if the central sprung clips become strained through overloading they will not stay closed when the display pages are turned.

It is possible to add a small amount of additional work into the portfolio at the front or back which does not depend on a sleeve for its display and therefore will not contribute to the overloading of the spring clips.

Before buying a display case make sure the portfolio will take all the mounts you have selected.

Materials

You will need the following:
- Cutting board or thick piece of waste carton or board.
- Cutting blade, Stanley knife or similar.
- Metal ruler.
- Set square.
- Kneadable or soft eraser.
- Pencils.
- Adhesives: Prit Stick or similar if the work is to be placed inside a display case; spray mount is best for loose card mounts.
- Access to a word processor and printer or dry lettering for headings and captions.
- Fine line pen: hand-written captions can be used to good effect if the above options are not available; lettering stencils can be obtained from art shops.
- Masking tape.
- Blue tac.
- Note pad or scrap paper.
- Mounting board.
- Assorted cartridge or medium weight paper.

Backing paper

Most portfolios with transparent display sleeves already have lightweight paper inside the plastic display pocket. It is usual to leave this paper inside and to place your own artwork on either side of it, mounted, if necessary, on the lightest and most appropriate card for your artwork.

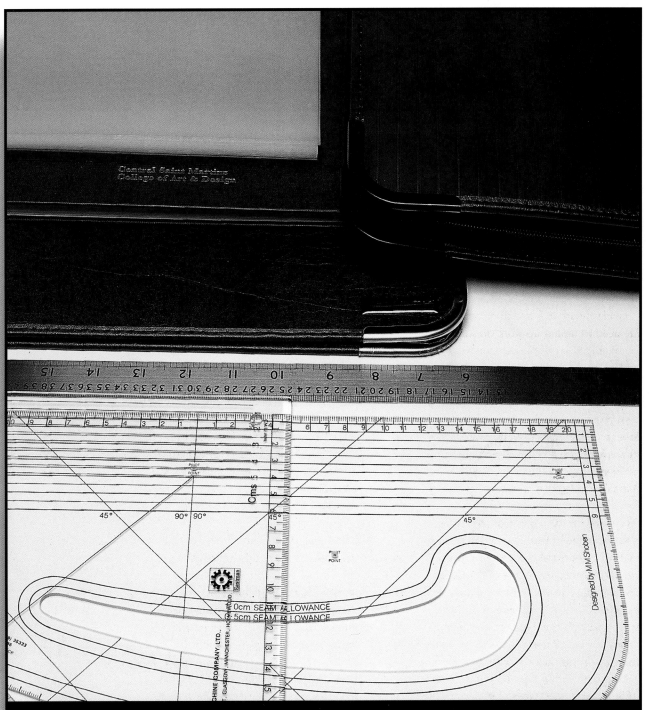

Portfolio display cases.

It is tempting to use a coloured paper or card as a backing mount but this can be a big mistake. If colours change for each project or even from page to page they distract from rather than enhance the work on display.

Choose one neutral colour that will work for every project such as a mid or light grey, cream or buff, or rely on the simplicity of black or white cartridge paper and lightweight board. Both black and white can be used as a backing mount in the same project and throughout the portfolio with stunning effect, but it is important not to alternate as the change can be very distracting.

This chapter assumes that all work will be flat-mounted so window mounts will not need to be cut.

Buy a small selection of card and paper from your usual art suppliers. Ask to see a range of lightweight mounting card and choose something that is adequately firm without being too thick or heavy. Initially, only buy enough paper and card to help plan the mounts. Specialist card is expensive: plan first, count up the number of sheets required then buy without excess or waste. Always check the size of the card and paper you have selected and make a note of the details and cost for future reference.

Remove one of the separating sheets from inside the display sleeves and, using this as a guide, trim your selection of paper and card to exactly the same size as the separating paper so that it slides into the display pocket easily.

Sorting out your work

Arrange all the same project work together, even if there is a piece which is not quite finished. Place all the research work with its relevant project or set of design drawings.

Sort through all your research files and notebooks, using book marks or paper clips to identify sections which are relevant to specific projects. Do not remove work from drawing books; simply mark it for future use.

Sort each set of work into the order in which it was generated.

Re-create the story of each project step by step, from the first research and drawings to the finished design and illustrations. Hunt for any missing sections and if you have selected an entire section as 'OUT', then retrieve it for the time being in order to have a complete project.

Sort out the photographs for each project and decide on the most appropriate for presentation. Identify the best and most useful with a mark on the reverse.

Depending on how much photographic material you have, either allocate the appropriate photographs to each project or, if there are only one or two for each, it might be better to mount all the photographs together so they form a separate section.

Label the photographs on the back according to the project to which they belong, separate them into envelopes and label the envelopes with an identifying title and the number of prints inside. Do not discard any at this stage.

If any of the photographs are exceptionally good you should make enlargements, if you haven't already. Find a nearby photo lab or colour photocopy shop and discover the amount of time needed for processing. You will need to calculate the funds at your disposal for this very costly section of the portfolio.

It is difficult to visualize how impressive a piece of work will look when mounted if it has fingerprints on areas that are meant to be clean or has curled and damaged edges. Although this is a tedious job, go through every piece of selected work and clean, trim and, if necessary, apply fixative. It is good practice to clean up the back of the work to prevent further transfer of dirt and, if a particular piece of work needs extra protection, cover it with a sheet of tracing or tissue paper held into place with masking tape.

Now is the time to begin planning the mounts for each section, project or story.

Set out 4-6 blank sheets of A2 paper. Count the number of projects. Allocate a set number of mounts to each section or division of work so that when they are all added together they do not exceed the maximum number of display pages that your portfolio can hold.

A compact, concise portfolio, full of the very best work, on display sheets which turn easily is your ultimate aim. So, allocate 2 or more display sheets per project eg in a 30-sided display portfolio

it could be possible to present between 7 and 10 separate sections of work.

In an uncluttered space spread all the work, including photographs, for one of the sections or projects out flat in sequence order so that the story of the project is before you in full. Place the appropriate work on top of the mounts. If the finished work warrants more mounts, then other material will have to be condensed and merged in order to save space.

It is important that you create a strong impact with your visual presentation. Keep the images uncluttered and allow at least a 2.5 cm border all round the mount. When you have finished, simply tack each item down to hold it in place temporarily. Make a note of the project or section number and the mount number together with the fact that the sheet is unfinished and untitled. Place all unused work inside a folded sheet of scrap paper and label it as spare work.

You have now told the story of your first project.

The reasons for the temporary fixing of artwork are twofold. Firstly, when starting to select and mount work it is difficult to visualize the finished presentation sheets, but after selecting and positioning twenty mounts, all with different images, it is often easier to be more creative and to take risks with the presentation. If every sheet has been loosely fixed into position it is simpler to go back to the early sheets and reposition work with the hindsight of having planned an entire portfolio.

The second reason is that on completing the preliminary presentation you may find you have too many sheets for your folder. In this case several may have to be taken out and the artwork possibly re-positioned on one of the remaining pages. Alternatively, you might be in the happy position of finding that some sections could take additional work and that the busier sheets of a section could be regrouped onto new mounts giving the images more space and the project, as a whole, a more expansive feel.

Remember to draw out a plan for each mount, number all sheets and keep accurate notes throughout.

Borders

Borders and spacing between items should have some uniformity. Try to make sure that all vertical and horizontal lines follow through and are parallel with one another. Keep all borders equal throughout a mount but allow more space at the bottom of the page.

Annotation

If you are presenting working drawings, they are more than likely to have notes of explanation at the side of them. Do not eliminate these. Tidy them up and check that the information is legible and spelt correctly.

Titles

Sections of work or individual projects need a title or heading so that viewers know exactly what it is they are looking at. For example, if it is the final design in a project then attention needs to be drawn to this. If a sentence of explanation needs to be added it is better to place it under the title and keep the lettering clear of the finished work.

Printed lettering from a word processor arranged as a label gives a very professional finish. Alternatively, the dry backed rubdown lettering that can be bought from an art shop or stationers will do the job equally well. If you are applying rubdown lettering plan the words and spacing in advance and always lay the lettering down on a separate piece of paper beforehand as if it were a label. Then cut it out and fix it with spray mount or similar adhesive.

If you have access to neither a word processor nor rubdown lettering then, without attempting to copy a particular lettering style, plan the space for the title on a separate piece of paper which will act as the label. Write the necessary information by hand in capitals with a fine pen or, alternatively, use a stencil. Cut this out and apply as the other labels discussed, without attempting to make too big a feature of the title. Position the label top right or left but not to the centre of your finished mount.

Always label the work after each section has been mounted as all the labels should be made at the same time, in the same style and with the same neutral backing paper. These should be positioned at the same level and, approximately, area of each sheet to create a feeling of order.

Colour and space

Introduce colour into a section which appears overwhelmingly black, white and grey. This will lift the aspect of the page into something which has a focal point of eye-catching interest.

This is a particularly useful device when presenting developmental drawings which are primarily in black on white. If the drawings are bold and powerful they should be left untouched although a colour border could be added without causing a distraction.

If the series of drawings is not quite bold enough and therefore not up to the eye-catching standard of other work then you can adapt them.

Decide on the most important images. If there are sections that would benefit from being enlarged, photocopy them and then add colour to the photocopied enlargements.

Alternatively, where a section contains a lot of eye-catching colour, certain parts might benefit from being made more subtle in order to aid clarity. This process is easier than adding colour and again requires you to select tissue paper and tracing paper of the lightest grey or off white. Do not select a sheet of coloured paper even if there is a colour which relates to your existing mount.

Space

Never cram images on to a mount. A cluttered page creates confusion because the eye cannot take in and understand all the information at once. The observer will focus on one section to begin with and follow this up by looking for more interesting detail as he or she gathers information about what is going on the page.

Remember that the portfolio is a document of communication and each section is telling a story about how you think, create ideas, apply your skills and resolve them into a design proposal. Use the space available to inform the observer about your skills and strong points.

If you draw in a precise and orderly way, then present your drawings in the same orderly manner to highlight this method. If the drawings you have selected are all variations on a theme, introduce an element from the theme and use the space of the sheet to emphasize this.

Collage

You will probably not have enough space on the presentation mounts to include all your research and background work. Reduce the research work for a project to one or two sheets by means of collage. These sheets can be included as separate mounts at the beginning of each project.

A collage is a gathering together of interesting, diverse and often unrelated items which serve to identify the purpose, starting point and exploration of a theme. The technique can be used to condense images into a smaller format, so allowing more images and a more comprehensive story of the project. Collage also permits you to regroup the sequence of the story.

The mounting of a collage must be precise, with no wrinkles or misaligned edges, or the overall effect can resemble a disorganized scrap book.

Keep the images, text, photographs and textures readable and presented in an interesting way so the relationship between source of inspiration and work can be clearly seen. Position the work temporarily until the entire project has been mounted so that images can be moved around if need be, then stick it down using adhesives appropriate for the materials selected. If necessary, title and annotate the collage. Do not place it in a plastic sleeve until the adhesive is thoroughly dry.

If you have clearly-ordered sheets of design work you should resist the temptation to collage mount and only use this method when absolutely necessary. In the case of a sheet of designs where one or two are not up to standard, it is possible to overmount more interesting images. Make sure when doing this that the image being overmounted does not show through.

General arrangement

The presented work has to communicate all aspects of your creativity. Therefore, it is important to look through the portfolio from beginning to end when all sorting, planning, annotating and titling is complete. This is the last opportunity to make adjustments that might alter the character of a section and, in turn, alter the profile of the entire portfolio.

Check that the work looks varied, that the colour and texture adds to the richness of each section and that notes and titles are brief but give sufficient information for the work to be understood in your absence.

Finally, check the running order. Decide whether or not you want variety by separating projects which are similar or to show a continuity of design by keeping them together.

Wall or board displays

Selecting work for display is not simply choosing the work with which you are happiest. Work mounted in an exhibition has to be both eye-catching and able to be clearly understood from a distance of approximately 2 to 3 metres.

You also have to make the choice of either showing a selection of work from across the whole portfolio, or, alternatively, showing the main mounted sheets from two of the most successful projects.

Whatever your decision, try these permutations. First, spread the chosen work out on a table or floor in the exact position you would like each piece to be. Keep all vertical lines and horizontal lines level and the spacing in-between each mount even. Draw out the display in a sketch book or on a sheet of paper that can be tucked into the portfolio pocket and identify each of the selected sheets by placing a coloured dot in the corner. If you are unsure of the space that you will be allocated then work out two or more variations using the above method for selection and, draw out each possible display and colour code the sheets accordingly.

If you are expected to display work as an exhibition have it all planned in advance and even take your own mounting pins and adhesives with you as a contingency measure.

Time management

After the sections have been prepared and temporarily fixed, make a planning chart of the time left to complete the mounting of the portfolio. If you have kept a notebook of the work to be done and a record of the page numbers and page plans this should be a relatively easy task.

Be realistic when you calculate the time you have to complete the work outlined in your notes. Do not plan to finish the portfolio preparation the night before the interview. Allow time to label the front, the spine and the inside of the portfolio sleeve with your name and address. Use this format for any 3D work and also for the sketch, drawing or research books that will accompany the portfolio to the interview.

Check your time planning chart at the start of each working session and write down a list of jobs that have to be done. Should anything remain unfinished then add the work to the next session but try at all costs to keep up with the plan. Some jobs will be faster and some slower than anticipated and you have to adjust your plan accordingly.

Selecting a course for further study

There are numerous fashion design courses to choose from. Some of the possibilities are listed below.

• General courses which cover all aspects of fashion and clothing production and usually give an opportunity to specialize in one or more areas of design.
• Industrial, manufacturing and clothing technology-based design courses which may have considerable links with industry and offer industrial liaison, sponsorship and work placements.
• Accessory design courses, for example, in millinery, footwear, jewellery and embroidery.
• Courses which combine fashion with textiles and that subject's many subdivisions (print, weave, knit, embroidery, technology and management).
• Courses which are specialist from the outset, such as contour fashion, tailoring, menswear, womenswear, knit, embroidery and textile conservation.
• Courses which link fashion to costume design for theatre, film and television.
• Courses which deal with fashion promotion, styling, make up, journalism, illustration, photography, retail, marketing, management and fashion development.
• Cross disciplinary courses which offer the opportunity to study fashion for a period of time within a much broader curriculum which could include sculpture, painting, ceramics, three-dimensional design, history of art and contextual studies.

If, as the time for your application draws nearer, you still have no clear idea as to which course to opt for, obtain a comprehensive guide to all the courses available (see p95) and go through it asking yourself the following questions – and be honest and realistic with your answers.

• How many years do you want to study?
• What exactly are your main interests in the subject?
• Is there a combination of subjects within an area that you find interesting; if so what are they?
• Are there any aspects or areas of study that do not hold your interest?
• Do you want a course that specializes in design with manufacture and involves learning about new technology?
• Would you prefer a course that has a strong business element as well as design and manufacture?
• Would you like to study how to manage, market and promote the designs of others?
• Would you prefer to study on a course which has a specified period in industry as part of your study?
• Do you want to study abroad as part of your course?
• Do you want to study on a course that allows you to study other subject areas?
• How essential is it for you to stay within reasonable travelling distance of your present home?

Alternatively, look through the various brochures which list courses in your subject area. If the title, details and location appeal to you, use a highlighter pen to mark the name of the college or institution concerned. Continue until you have covered all the options. Then apply the checklist from the previous section to each highlighted choice and eliminate those that do not match your requirements.

Remember that it should be the type of course that appeals to you most, not its location, past reputation or the fact that you know someone there, that influences your decision.

On completing a shortlist, contact each college and request the relevant course brochures. It is vitally important to try to visit all of your final choices; the majority will have access and open days especially for prospective candidates. Open Days usually take place early in the Spring Term, although this can vary. Most courses advise you to contact them beforehand as numbers are often restricted for safety and security purposes. A senior member of staff or Course Leader may give an illustrated presentation of the course to visitors at a pre-booked time.

Before visiting a college, draw up a list of questions covering the facilities on offer, access to amenities which are important to you, or things that were unclear in the course literature. Ask about past student successes, what companies they have gone on to work for and, most importantly, the level at which they started their employment! You must ask about recent course changes as some options may have been at the development stage when the prospectus was being prepared.

Questions to ask include:
- Will you interview all the applicants or will you pre-select from the application forms?
- How many places do you leave open for second and subsequent choice candidates?
- How much work do you expect to see in a portfolio?
- Do you ask interviewees to mount an exhibition of their work; if so, approximately how much space do you allow for each candidate?
- Do you interview each person with or without their work?
- Should I bring any 3-D work with me or would you prefer photographs/transparencies?
- Should I bring all my sketch and research books with me or should I pre-select some; if so, how many would you like to see?
- If I have transparencies of my 3-D work will there be facilities for me to show them? Use this question to find out about audio visual facilities if you need them.
- Do the interviewees have any written work to do on the day of the interview?
- Does the course require a piece of written work as part of the portfolio?

- Do the interviews for this course last the whole day? (important if there is a lot of travelling involved)
- Do the candidates have to bring proof of past exam passes with them on the day of the interview?

If any of these questions appear troublesome or embarrassing and there are several of you visiting the same course, divide the questions amongst the group, but remember to take note of all the answers.

Some courses will pre-empt all these questions and include the answers to most of them in a prepared hand out or talk. Other courses will fully brief an applicant by letter.

When you are at the interview remember that the interviewer is only interested in being able to find out more about you. Every effort will be made to put you at your ease. The atmosphere in the variety of interviews that I have been involved with has been relaxed and informal enough for even the most timid or nervous to feel comfortable.

On the day of the interview make sure that you arrive early with adequate time to prepare yourself and your work without the added stress of a last minute rush or apologies for being late. If you are unfortunate enough to have been seriously delayed by transport then telephone ahead at the earliest opportunity in order to let the interview team know of your delay. This enables interview times to be rescheduled.

Success or failure: what next?

If your application has been unsuccessful, swift decisions can still secure you a place on another course. What is vital is that you do not admit defeat and that you continue with the system that has been set up to assist you through this difficult time.

If you were given any feedback about your work at the first unsuccessful interview it is time to consider carefully exactly what was said. You need to analyse all the comments that were made and, if any were negative, to make sure that these are considered and turned into positive points before the next interview.

The most positive thing to do before a second interview is to begin some totally fresh work. A new project or series of drawings, which need not be completed before the next interview, can look very impressive in a portfolio. The work should be simply presented, unmounted, in a section or loose folder slotted into the back of the portfolio and labelled 'work in progress'. The professional and disciplined attitude of someone who has taken the trouble not only to re-work sections of a portfolio but to generate new work as well is bound to impress.

If, however, after all attempts you are still unsuccessful, think long and hard about attempting to re-apply at a later date unless you have access to part-time tuition. A new application will involve a re-appraisal of existing work, a submission of new project work and a complete re-think about the most appropriate course. It would be advisable to have some professional guidance on all these decisions.

The future

The creative work of a graduating student can be so ahead of its time that the student is forced to work without any industrial or financial backing in the hope that their designs will eventually achieve a degree of recognition or fame.

Some graduating students will choose a further course of study in order to specialize in a particular area before seeking employment; others prefer to develop business or academic skills in order to promote creativity in others.

Established fashion and promotional companies always visit the graduation shows, and are ready to offer employment to those whose work suits their needs.

The tendency over the past few years has been for courses to offer more choices and individual routes for specialism by adopting modular or combination structures. This way of working can really benefit the student who has broader interests and may lead to wider career opportunities in the future.

Increasingly, industrial and commercial links are enabling students to benefit much more, not only from sponsorship of materials and final year shows, but also by offering work placement schemes and provide considerable opportunities for experience and for making contacts for future employment.

Many courses have built considerable international links during the past few years, either for work placement opportunities or for more adventurous course exchange networks. All this information should be available either in the individual course brochures or on the Internet. International linking, learning and cross continent resourcing could become the norm for most graduates from creative courses rather than something experienced only by a lucky minority.

Several of the students whose Foundation and First Year work has been used as illustrations in earlier chapters in this book have now completed their courses and are out working in the international arena.

Further information

Addresses

UCAS (Universities and Colleges
Admissions Service)
Fulton House,
Jessop Avenue,
Cheltenham,
Gloucestershire GL50 35H
Tel: 01242 2224449 (main line)
Tel: 01242 227788 (general enquiries)

Careers & Occupational Information
Centre
PO Box 308
Bristol BS99 7FE
Tel: 0117 9777199
Fax: 0117 9724509

National Council for Vocational
Qualifications
(NCVQ)
222 Euston Road
London NW1 2BZ
Tel: 0171 387 9898
Fax: 0171 387 0978

National Society for Education in Art &
Design
The Gatehouse
Carsham Court
Carsham
Wiltshire SN13 0BZ
Tel: 01249 714825
Fax: 01249 716138

National Union of Students
Nelson Mandela House
461 Holloway Road
London N7 6LJ
Tel: 0171 272 8900
Fax: 0171 263 5713

Open College of the Arts
Houndhill
Warsbrough
Barnsley
South Yorkshire S70 6TU
Tel: 01226 730495
Fax: 01226 730838

Open University
Walton Hall
Milton Keynes MK7 6AA
Tel: 01908 274066
Fax: 01908 652099

Scottish Vocational Education Council
Hanover House
24 Douglas Street
Glasgow G2 7NQ
Tel: 0141 242 2168
Fax: 0141 242 2244

SKILL - National Bureau for Students
with Disabilities
336 Brixton Road
London SW9 7AA
Tel: 0171 274 0565 (general enquiries)
Tel: 0171 978 9890
Fax: 0171 274 7840

Reading list

Allen, Anne and Seaman, Julian, *Fashion
Drawing: The Basic Principles*, BT
Batsford Ltd, 1993

Ireland, Patrick, *Introduction to Fashion
Design*, BT Batsford Ltd, 1992

Seaman, Julian, *Fashion Illustration:
Basic Techniques*, BT Batsford Ltd, 1996

Seaman, Julian, *Professional Fashion
Illustration*, BT Batsford Ltd, 1995

UCAS, *On Course: The Official Directory of
Art and Design Courses*

Index